INDIAN COOKBOOK

RAITA AND CROQUETTE

RECIPES

Traditional, Creative and Delicious
Indian Recipes Easily To prepare

Akhila Aggarwal

Copyright © 2021 by Akhila Aggarwal

Legal Disclaimer

TABLE OF CONTENTS

INDIAN RAITA AND CROQUETTE RECIPES

Simple Salt and Pepper Raita

***Servings:* 4 to 6 servings**

INGREDIENTS:

- ✓ ⅓ teaspoon salt, or to taste
- ✓ 3 cups non-fat plain yogurt, whisked until the desired smoothness is achieved
- ✓ Freshly ground mixed peppercorns, such as red, black, green, and white, to taste

DIRECTIONS:

1. In a serving container, combine the yogurt, salt, and half the mixed peppercorns.

2. Sprinkle the rest of the pepper on top as a decoration, and refrigerate until ready to serve.

Ginger and Scallion Raita

Servings: **4 to 6 servings**

INGREDIENTS:

- ✓ ⅓ teaspoon salt, or to taste
- ✓ ½ teaspoon ground paprika
- ✓ 1 fresh green chile pepper, such as serrano, minced with seeds
- ✓ 1 teaspoon sugar
- ✓ 1 to 2 tablespoons minced fresh mint leaves
- ✓ 1½ tablespoons peeled minced fresh ginger
- ✓ 3 cups non-fat plain yogurt, whisked until the desired smoothness is achieved
- ✓ 5 to 6 scallions, white and light green parts, minced

DIRECTIONS:

1. In a serving container, combine the yogurt, ginger, scallions, sugar, and salt.

2. Garnish with paprika and mint before you serve.

Iced Raita

Servings:4 to 6 servings

INGREDIENTS:

✓ ¼ teaspoon salt, or to taste

✓ 1 cup crushed ice (kept chilled)

✓ 3 cups non-fat plain yogurt, whisked until the desired smoothness is achieved

✓ Freshly ground black pepper, to taste

DIRECTIONS:

1. Mix everything together in a big container and serve instantly.

Lemon Pickle Raita

***Servings:*4 to 6 servings**

INGREDIENTS:

- ✓ 1 tablespoon Crushed Lemon and Fresh Red Chile Pepper Pickle
- ✓ 2 to 3 tablespoons snipped chives
- ✓ 3 cups non-fat plain yogurt, whisked until the desired smoothness is achieved

DIRECTIONS:

1. Ready the pickle. Next, place the yogurt in a serving container and stir in the lemon pickle. Add salt and pepper, if required.

2. Put in the chives and stir mildly to combine, with some of them visible as a decoration.

Beet and Scallion Raita

Servings:4 to 6 servings

INGREDIENTS:

- ✓ four to five scallions, minced
- ✓ ½ teaspoon freshly ground black pepper, or to taste
- ✓ ½ teaspoon salt, or to taste
- ✓ 1 fresh green chile pepper, such as serrano, minced with seeds
- ✓ 1 teaspoon minced fresh garlic
- ✓ 2 cups non-fat plain yogurt, whisked until the desired smoothness is achieved
- ✓ 2 tablespoons finely chopped cilantro
- ✓ 3 medium beets

DIRECTIONS:

1. Put the beets in a small pan with water to cover by 2 inches and bring to a boil using high heat. Decrease the heat to moderate to low, cover the pan, and simmer until tender, approximately fifteen minutes. Turn off the heat, allow to cool down, then peel and cut finely. Let sit for about 1 tablespoon for garnish.

2. Put the yogurt in a serving dish and stir in the beets, scallions, garlic, green chile pepper, salt, and black pepper. Garnish with the reserved beets and the cilantro before you serve.

Cucumber and Radish Raita

Servings:4 to 6 servings

INGREDIENTS:

- ✓ ½ teaspoon freshly ground black pepper, or to taste
- ✓ ½ teaspoon ground paprika
- ✓ ½ teaspoon salt, or to taste
- ✓ 1 fresh green chile pepper, such as serrano, minced with seeds
- ✓ 1 large firm tomato, finely chopped
- ✓ 1 teaspoon Chaat Masala (Homemade or store-bought)
- ✓ 2 cups non-fat plain yogurt, whisked until the desired smoothness is achieved
- ✓ 2 to 4 seedless cucumbers, grated (peeled or unpeeled)
- ✓ Cilantro or mint leaves
- ✓ twelve to fifteen red radishes, grated and squeezed

DIRECTIONS:

1. Ready the chaat masala. Put the yogurt in a serving container. Put in the cucumbers, radishes, tomato, green chile pepper, chaat masala, salt, and pepper and stir to mix thoroughly.

2. Garnish with the paprika and cilantro or mint leaves before you serve.

Kashmiri Morel Mushroom Raita

***Servings:*4 to 6 servings**

INGREDIENTS:

- ✓ ¼ cup finely chopped fresh cilantro
- ✓ 1 medium onion, cut in half along the length and thinly chopped
- ✓ 1 medium russet potato
- ✓ 1 tablespoon vegetable oil
- ✓ 2½ teaspoons Kashmiri Raita Masala
- ✓ 3 cups non-fat plain yogurt, whisked until the desired smoothness is achieved
- ✓ 8 to 10 large fresh or dried reconstituted morel mushrooms, thinly chopped
- ✓ Salt, to taste

DIRECTIONS:

1. Boil the potato in lightly salted water to cover until tender, then peel it and finely cut it. While it's cooking, ready the raita masala. Next, place the yogurt in a big serving container and stir in 2 teaspoons raita masala. Add salt, if required (there is already some in the masala).

2. Heat the oil in a small-sized non-stick skillet using moderate to high heat and cook the onion, stirring,

until a golden colour is achieved, approximately two to three minutes. Put in the potato and cook, stirring, approximately one minute, then put in the morel mushrooms and cilantro and cook another minute. Move to the yogurt, and mix thoroughly. Garnish with the rest of the ½ teaspoon raita masala and serve.

Mustard Seed Raita

Servings:4 to 6 servings

INGREDIENTS:

- ✓ ¼ cup finely chopped fresh cilantro
- ✓ ½ teaspoon salt, or to taste
- ✓ 1 small red onion, finely chopped
- ✓ 1 tablespoon black mustard seeds
- ✓ 1 tablespoon yellow or brown mustard seeds
- ✓ 1 to 2 teaspoons mustard oil or peanut oil
- ✓ 3 to 4 pickling cucumbers, peeled and finely chopped
- ✓ 4 cups non-fat plain yogurt, whisked until the desired smoothness is achieved

DIRECTIONS:

1. In a mortar and pestle or a spice grinder, crudely grind all the mustard seeds. Transfer to a small non-reactive container and stir in approximately ½ cup yogurt and the salt. Set aside to ferment at least 4 and maximum 1two hours at room temperature.

2. Put the yogurt in a big serving container and stir in the fermented mustard seed mixture. Stir in the

cucumbers and onions. Swirl in the mustard oil, garnish with the cilantro before you serve.

Potato and Beet Raita

Servings: 4 to 6 servings

INGREDIENTS:

- ✓ ⅓ teaspoon salt, or to taste
- ✓ 1 tablespoon peeled minced fresh ginger
- ✓ 1 tablespoon sesame seeds
- ✓ 1 teaspoon cumin seeds
- ✓ 1 teaspoon sugar
- ✓ 1 to 2 tablespoons fresh lemon juice
- ✓ 2 cups non-fat plain yogurt, whisked until the desired smoothness is achieved
- ✓ 2 small beets
- ✓ 3 small russet potatoes

DIRECTIONS:

1. Put the potatoes and beets in a small sauce-pan with water to cover and bring to a boil using high heat. Decrease the heat to moderate to low, cover the pan, and simmer until tender, approximately fifteen minutes. Turn off the heat, allow to cool down, then peel and cut them finely.

2. While the beets and potatoes are cooking, place the sesame and cumin seeds in a small-sized non-stick saucepan and dry-roast using moderate to high

heat until they are fragrant and seems slightly darker, approximately two minutes. Allow to cool, then grind crudely in a mortar and pestle or a spice grinder.

3. Put the yogurt in a big serving container. Stir in the lemon juice, ginger, sugar, salt, and half the sesame seeds. Stir in the potatoes and fold in the beets. Sprinkle the rest of the sesame seeds and the cumin seeds on top and serve.

Potato and Cumin Raita

Servings:4 to 6 servings

INGREDIENTS:

✓ ⅓ teaspoon salt, or to taste

✓ ½ cup minced chives or scallion greens

✓ ½ red bell pepper, finely chopped

✓ ½ teaspoon black peppercorns, or to taste

✓ 1 large russet potato

✓ 1¼ teaspoons cumin seeds

✓ 2½ cups non-fat plain yogurt, whisked until the desired smoothness is achieved

DIRECTIONS:

1. Boil the potato in lightly salted water to cover until tender, then peel it, and cut it finely. Next, place the cumin and black peppercorns in a small-sized non-stick saucepan and dry-roast using moderate to high heat until they are fragrant and seems slightly darker, approximately two minutes. Allow to cool, then grind crudely in a mortar and pestle or a spice grinder.

2. Put the yogurt in a serving container, stir in the potato, salt, and half the ground cumin-pepper mixture.

3. Put in the chives and stir mildly to combine, with a few of them visible as a decoration. Top with the rest of the cumin-pepper mixture, scatter the red bell pepper over everything before you serve.

Potato-Mustard Raita

Servings:4 to 6 servings

INGREDIENTS:

- ✓ ¼ teaspoon salt, or to taste
- ✓ 1 cup crudely chopped fresh cilantro, including soft stems
- ✓ 1 cup crudely chopped fresh spinach leaves
- ✓ 1 large russet potato
- ✓ 1 teaspoon cumin seeds
- ✓ 1 teaspoon ground pomegranate seeds
- ✓ 2 cups non-fat plain yogurt, whisked until the desired smoothness is achieved
- ✓ 3 to 4 scallions, crudely chopped

DIRECTIONS:

1. Boil the potato in lightly salted water to cover until tender, then peel it, and cut it finely. Next, place the cumin in a small-sized non-stick saucepan and dry-roast using moderate to high heat until they are fragrant and seems slightly darker, approximately two minutes. Allow to cool, then grind crudely in a mortar and pestle or a spice grinder. Next, place the yogurt in a big serving container; stir in the potato.

2. Using a food processor a blender, combine and pulse the spinach, cilantro, and scallions until puréed. Move to the yogurt. Put in the salt, pomegranate seeds, and half the cumin and mix thoroughly. Sprinkle the rest of the cumin on top and stir mildly with a fork, with most of it visible as a decoration. Serve.

Sprouted Beans and Vegetable Raita

Servings:4 to 6 servings

INGREDIENTS:

- ✓ ¼ cup finely chopped fresh cilantro, including soft stems

- ✓ ½ cup sprouted split mung beans (mung dal) (Homemade or store-bought)

- ✓ ½ teaspoon freshly ground black pepper, or to taste

- ✓ ½ teaspoon salt, or to taste

- ✓ 1 cup sprouted red lentils (Homemade or store-bought)

- ✓ 1 fresh green chile pepper, such as serrano, minced with seeds

- ✓ 1 small tomato, finely chopped

- ✓ 1 teaspoon Chaat Masala (Homemade or store-bought)

- ✓ 1 teaspoon dry-roasted sesame seeds

- ✓ 1 to 4 seedless cucumbers, grated (peeled or unpeeled)

- ✓ 2 cups non-fat plain yogurt, whisked until the desired smoothness is achieved

DIRECTIONS:

1. Ready the beans and lentils in advance. Ready the sesame seeds and chaat masala.

2. Put the yogurt in a big serving container. Stir in everything except 2 tablespoons of the red lentils, the sesame seeds, and the chaat masala. Sprinkle the reserved red lentils and sesame seeds on top, top with the chaat masala before you serve.

Tomato and Mint Leaves Raita

Servings: 4 to 6 servings

INGREDIENTS:

- ✓ ¼ cup finely chopped fresh mint leaves
- ✓ ¼ teaspoon crudely ground black pepper
- ✓ ½ teaspoon cumin seeds
- ✓ ½ teaspoon salt, or to taste
- ✓ 1 large tomato, finely chopped
- ✓ 1 teaspoon minced fresh garlic
- ✓ 2 cups non-fat plain yogurt, whisked until the desired smoothness is achieved
- ✓ 3 to 4 scallions, green parts only, thinly chopped

DIRECTIONS:

1. Put the sesame and cumin seeds in a small-sized non-stick saucepan and dry-roast using moderate to high heat until they are fragrant and seems slightly darker, approximately two minutes. Allow to cool, then grind crudely in a mortar and pestle or a spice grinder.

2. Put the yogurt in a serving dish and stir in the mint, tomato, scallions, garlic, and salt. Sprinkle black pepper and cumin on top and stir mildly to

combine, with parts of them visible as a decoration. Serve.

Fresh Spinach Raita with Ginger-Lime Pickle

Servings:4 to 6 servings

INGREDIENTS:

✓ ⅓ teaspoon freshly ground black pepper, or to taste

✓ ⅓ teaspoon salt, or to taste

✓ 1 small bunch (8 to 10 ounces) fresh spinach, trimmed of roots only, washed and finely chopped

✓ 1 tablespoon Minced Ginger-Lime Pickle

✓ 1 teaspoon dry-roasted and crudely ground cumin seeds

✓ 2½ cups non-fat plain yogurt, whisked until the desired smoothness is achieved

DIRECTIONS:

1. Ready the ginger-lime pickle in advance. Ready the cumin seeds. Next, place the yogurt in a serving container. Put in the spinach, ginger-lime pickle, salt, and black pepper, and stir to mix.

2. Lightly swirl in the cumin seeds, with parts of them visible as a decoration before you serve.

Frozen Spinach Raita

Servings:4 to 6 servings

INGREDIENTS:

- ✓ ¼ teaspoon black mustard seeds
- ✓ ¼ teaspoon ground black salt (not compulsory)
- ✓ ¼ teaspoon salt, or to taste
- ✓ ¼ teaspoon whole cumin seeds + 1 teaspoon dry-roasted and crudely ground cumin seeds
- ✓ 1 (10-ounce) package thawed frozen spinach (reserve all juices)
- ✓ 1 small onion, finely chopped
- ✓ 1 teaspoon olive oil
- ✓ 1 teaspoon peeled minced fresh ginger
- ✓ 3 cups non-fat plain yogurt, whisked until the desired smoothness is achieved
- ✓ A scant pinch ground asafoetida

DIRECTIONS:

1. Ready the roasted cumin seeds. Next, place the yogurt in a serving container. Stir in the salt and black salt.

2. Heat the oil in a small saucepan using moderate to high heat. Put in the mustard seeds and ¼

teaspoon whole cumin seeds; they should sizzle when they touch the hot oil. Swiftly stir in the asafoetida, then the onion and ginger, and cook, stirring, until a golden colour is achieved, approximately three minutes.

3. Put in the spinach plus all the juices and cook until most of the fluids vaporize, approximately four minutes. Allow to cool, then stir well into the yogurt. Mix half the roasted cumin into the yogurt, sprinkle the rest of the on top before you serve.

Green Raita

Servings:4 to 6 servings

INGREDIENTS:

- ✓ ½ cup crudely chopped fresh cilantro, including soft stems
- ✓ ½ teaspoon salt, or to taste
- ✓ 1 cup finely chopped yellow and red tomatoes
- ✓ 1 cup firmly packed fresh watercress leaves
- ✓ 1 fresh green chile pepper, such as serrano, stemmed
- ✓ 1 teaspoon dry-roasted and crudely ground cumin seeds
- ✓ 2 to 3 cups non-fat plain yogurt, whisked until the desired smoothness is achieved
- ✓ 3 large scallions, crudely chopped
- ✓ Freshly ground black pepper, to taste

DIRECTIONS:

1. Ready the cumin seeds. Next, Using a food processor or a blender, combine and pulse the scallions, green chile pepper, cilantro, and watercress until a smooth purée is achieved.

2. Put the yogurt in a serving container and stir in the puréed greens and salt. Pile up the tomatoes in the

center. (Do not mix them into the raita.) Sprinkle the roasted cumin and black pepper on top before you serve.

Sautéed Spinach Raita

Servings:4 to 6 servings

INGREDIENTS:

- ✓ ¼ cup roasted peanuts, crudely chopped
- ✓ ½ teaspoon salt, or to tasteFreshly ground black pepper, to taste
- ✓ 1 small bunch fresh spinach (8 to 10 ounces), trimmed of roots only, washed and finely chopped,
- ✓ 1 tablespoon peeled minced fresh ginger
- ✓ 1 tablespoon vegetable oil
- ✓ 1 teaspoon dry-roasted and crudely ground cumin seeds (See the dry-roasting section in Introduction)
- ✓ 1 teaspoon minced fresh garlic
- ✓ 1 teaspoon sesame seeds, dry-roasted (See the dry-roasting section in Introduction)
- ✓ 3 cups non-fat plain yogurt, whisked until the desired smoothness is achieved

DIRECTIONS:

1. Ready the cumin and sesame seeds. Next, heat the oil in a big non-stick wok or saucepan using moderate to high heat and cook the ginger and garlic, stirring, until a golden colour is achieved,

approximately one minute. Put in the spinach and cook, stirring, until completely wilted and slightly golden, three to five minutes. Set aside to cool.

2. Put the yogurt in a serving container. Put in the salt, then stir in the cooled spinach, plus any juices that may have accumulated.

3. Lightly swirl in the cumin and sesame seeds, and the black pepper, with parts of them visible as a decoration. Sprinkle the peanuts on top andserve.

Spicy Raita with Lamb's Quarters

Servings: **4 to 6 servings**

INGREDIENTS:

- ✓ ¼ teaspoon salt, or to taste
- ✓ 1 fresh green chile pepper, such as serrano, minced with seeds
- ✓ 1 teaspoon cumin seeds
- ✓ 1 to 2 teaspoons olive oil
- ✓ 2 cups finely chopped lamb's quarters leaves
- ✓ 2 cups non-fat plain yogurt, whisked until the desired smoothness is achieved
- ✓ 3 to 4 scallions, green parts only, finely chopped
- ✓ Freshly ground black pepper, to taste

DIRECTIONS:

1. Put the leaves in a big saucepan of water to cover using high heat and bring to a boil. Boil until soft, about four to five minutes. Another way is to cover and cook in a microwave-safe dish on high, approximately two to three minutes.

2. Allow to cool. Move to a food processor and pulse until crudely chopped, or cut by hand.

3. Put the yogurt in a serving dish and softly stir in the greens. Put in the scallions, salt, and black pepper, and mix once more.

4. Heat the oil in a small saucepan using moderate to high heat and put in the chile pepper and cumin seeds; they should sizzle when they touch the hot oil. Swiftly put them in to the yogurt, swirl lightly before you serve.

Tofu and Greens Mix Raita

Servings:4 to 6 servings

INGREDIENTS:

- ✓ ¼ teaspoon salt, or to taste
- ✓ ½ cup crudely chopped fresh cilantro, including soft stems
- ✓ ½ teaspoon Roasted Cumin-Pepper Masala
- ✓ 1 (10½-ounce) package firm tofu, towel-dried and crudely crumbled
- ✓ 1 cup crudely chopped fresh dry spinach leaves, rinsed and blotted
- ✓ 1 fresh green chile pepper, such as serrano, minced with seeds
- ✓ 1 tablespoon peeled minced fresh ginger
- ✓ 1½ cups non-fat plain yogurt, whisked until the desired smoothness is achieved
- ✓ 4 to 6 scallions, white parts only, minced

DIRECTIONS:

1. Ready the masala. Next, Using a food processor or blender, combine and pulse the tofu, spinach, and cilantro until the desired smoothness is achieved.

2. Move to a serving container, stir in the yogurt, ginger, scallions, chile pepper, and salt. Garnish with the cumin-pepper masala and serve.

Tofu and Mint Chutney Raita

Servings:4 to 6 servings

INGREDIENTS:

- ✓ ½ teaspoon salt, or to taste
- ✓ 1 (10½-ounce) package firm tofu, towel-dried and crudely crumbled
- ✓ 1 large red bell pepper, stemmed, seeded, and finely chopped
- ✓ 1 teaspoon Chaat Masala (Homemade or store-bought)
- ✓ 1½ cups non-fat plain yogurt, whisked until the desired smoothness is achieved
- ✓ 2 tablespoons Mint Chutney with Pomegranate Seeds

DIRECTIONS:

1. Ready the chutney and the chaat masala. Next, place the yogurt in a big serving container and stir in the chutney, chaat masala, and salt.

2. Put in the tofu and mix once more. Garnish with the red bell pepper and serve.

Banana Raita

Servings:4 to 6 servings

INGREDIENTS:

- ✓ ¼ cup any sonth chutney of your choice
- ✓ ¼ cup chopped raw almonds
- ✓ ¼ teaspoon salt, or to taste
- ✓ ½ teaspoon dry-roasted and crudely ground cumin seeds (See the dry-roasting section in Introduction)
- ✓ ½ teaspoon freshly ground black pepper, or to taste
- ✓ 1 tablespoon sugar
- ✓ 2 cups non-fat plain yogurt, whisked until the desired smoothness is achieved
- ✓ 2 small ripe bananas, peeled and chopped diagonally

DIRECTIONS:

1. Ready the chutney and the cumin seeds. Next, place the yogurt in a container and stir in the sugar, salt, black pepper, and half the almonds.

2. Gently stir in the bananas. Next, swirl in the sonth chutney, sprinkle the cumin seeds and the rest of the almonds on top before you serve.

Dried Fruit Raita

Servings:4 to 6 servings

INGREDIENTS:

- ✓ ¼ cup any sonth chutney of your choice
- ✓ ½ cup finely chopped fresh cilantro, including soft stems
- ✓ ½ cup lowfat milk
- ✓ ½ teaspoon freshly ground black pepper
- ✓ ½ teaspoon salt, or to taste
- ✓ 1 cup finely chopped mixed dried fruit, such as peaches, plums, apricots, and raisins
- ✓ 1 teaspoon Chaat Masala (Homemade or store-bought)
- ✓ 2 cups non-fat plain yogurt, whisked until the desired smoothness is achieved

DIRECTIONS:

1. Ready the chutney and the masala. Next, place the milk and the dried fruits in a microwave-safe container and cook on high, approximately one minute. Cover the container and allow the dried fruits to soften, approximately one hour. Allow to cool, then move them, with the liquid, to a serving container.

2. Put in the yogurt, salt, pepper, and cilantro, and mix thoroughly. Lightly swirl in the sonth chutney, with parts of it visible as a decoration. Sprinkle the chaat masala on top and serve.

Mandarin Orange Raita

Servings:4 to 6

INGREDIENTS:

- ✓ ¼ cup shelled and crudely chopped raw peanuts, without the red skin
- ✓ ¼ teaspoon salt, or to taste
- ✓ 1 cup canned mandarin orange segments, drained well
- ✓ 1 tablespoon peeled minced fresh ginger
- ✓ 1 teaspoon Chaat Masala (Homemade or store-bought)
- ✓ 2 cups non-fat plain yogurt, whisked until the desired smoothness is achieved
- ✓ 2 tablespoons finely chopped fresh mint leaves
- ✓ 2 teaspoons Chile Pepper Paste, or to taste

DIRECTIONS:

1. Ready the chile paste and the chaat masala. Next, place the yogurt in a serving container and stir in the chile paste, chaat masala, and salt. Fold in the mandarin segments, ginger, and mint leaves.

2. Put the peanuts in a small skillet and roast using moderate heat until it begins to look golden and releases its fragrance, approximately two minutes. Scatter over the yogurt mixture and serve.

43

Mango Chutney Raita

Servings:4 to 6 servings

INGREDIENTS:

- ✓ ½ cup Fragrant Mango Chutney Preserve
- ✓ 2 cups non-fat plain yogurt, whisked until the desired smoothness is achieved
- ✓ 2 tablespoons Dessert Masala

DIRECTIONS:

1. Ready the mango chutney and the dessert masala. Next, Using a food processor or blender, combine and pulse the chutney and 1 cup yogurt until the desired smoothness is achieved.

2. Transfer to a serving container and stir in the rest of the yogurt. Put in the dessert masala and stir mildly to combine, with parts of it visible as a decoration.

Mango-Ginger Raita

Servings:4 to 6 servings

INGREDIENTS:

- ✓ ½ teaspoon freshly ground black pepper, or to taste
- ✓ ½ teaspoon salt, or to taste
- ✓ 1 fresh green chile pepper, such as serrano, minced with seeds
- ✓ 1 tablespoon fresh lemon juice
- ✓ 1 tablespoon peeled minced fresh ginger
- ✓ 2 cups non-fat plain yogurt, whisked until the desired smoothness is achieved
- ✓ 2 large soft ripe mangoes

DIRECTIONS:

1. Cut or peel off the skin of the mangoes, then cut around the seed to make 2 cheeks of the flesh. Cut this fruit and the other fruit left near the seed into ½-inch pieces. Put three-quarters of the pieces in a shallow serving dish. Crudely mash the rest of the quarter with a fork to make a textured, chunky sauce, and set the sauce aside.

2. To the mango chunks, put in the yogurt, ginger, lemon juice, green chile pepper, salt, and black

pepper, and mix gently. Drizzle the mango sauce on top and serve.

Crispy Chickpea Batter Drops Raita

Servings:4 to 6

INGREDIENTS:

✓ ¼ cup finely chopped fresh cilantro, including soft stems

✓ ¼ teaspoon salt, or to taste

✓ ½ teaspoon freshly ground black pepper, or to taste

✓ ½ teaspoon ground paprika for garnish

✓ 1 teaspoon dry-roasted and crudely ground cumin seeds

✓ 2 cups non-fat plain yogurt, whisked until the desired smoothness is achieved

✓ 2 cups savory Crispy Chickpea Batter Drops (Boondi) or store-bought

DIRECTIONS:

1. Ready the boondi and the cumin. Next, place the yogurt in a serving container and stir in the salt, black pepper, cumin, and paprika.

2. Lightly stir in the boondi with some of them visible as garnish (or just mound them all on top). Sprinkle the cilantro on top and serve instantly (or the boondi will get soggy).

Crispy Urad Dal Croquettes in Yogurt

Servings:4 to 6 servings

INGREDIENTS:

- ✓ ¼ cup any sonth chutney of your choice, such as Minty Sonth Chutney with Mango Powder and Jaggery
- ✓ ¼ teaspoon salt, or to taste
- ✓ ½ cup lowfat milk
- ✓ ½ teaspoon cayenne pepper, or to taste
- ✓ ½ teaspoon freshly ground black pepper, or to taste
- ✓ ½ to 1 cup Fresh Coconut Chutney with Cilantro
- ✓ 1 tablespoon minced fresh cilantro, including soft stems
- ✓ 1 tablespoon minced fresh green mint leaves
- ✓ 1 teaspoon cumin seeds, dry-roasted and crudely ground (See the dry-roasting section in Introduction)
- ✓ 1 to 2 fresh green chile peppers, such as serrano, minced with seeds
- ✓ 2 teaspoons New Delhi Street Food Masala (Papri Masala)or to taste

✓ 3 cups non-fat plain yogurt, whisked until the desired smoothness is achieved

✓ 5 to 6 (½ recipe) Mung Bean Croquettes

DIRECTIONS:

1. Ready the croquettes, cumin, masala, and chutneys in advance, if possible. Put the yogurt in a big serving dish, stir in the coconut chutney, milk, salt, black pepper, cayenne pepper, and roasted cumin, and refrigerate until needed.

2. An hour before you serve, cut each croquette in half across the width and add to the yogurt. Mix softly until all of the croquettes are coated thoroughly with yogurt. Drizzle the sonth chutney on top. Garnish with the masala, green chile peppers, mint, and cilantro before you serve.

Mung Bean Croquettes Raita

Servings:4 to 6 servings

INGREDIENTS:

- ✓ ½ teaspoon freshly ground pepper, or to taste

- ✓ ½ teaspoon salt, or to taste

- ✓ 1 fresh green chile pepper, such as serrano, minced with seeds

- ✓ 16 to 20 (1 recipe) Mung Bean Croquettes

- ✓ 2 tablespoons finely chopped fresh cilantro, with soft stems

- ✓ 2 teaspoons dry-roasted and crudely ground cumin seeds (See the dry-roasting section in Introduction)

- ✓ 3 cups water for soaking the croquettes

- ✓ 3 to 4 cups non-fat plain yogurt, whisked until the desired smoothness is achieved

DIRECTIONS:

1. Ready the cumin seeds and the croquettes. Next, place the yogurt in a big serving container, stir in the salt, black pepper, and 1 teaspoon cumin seeds, and refrigerate until needed.

2. An hour before you serve, put the water in a big saucepan, bring to a boil, then remove from the heat and soak the croquettes until they absorb the

water and become soft, approximately two to three minutes. Press lightly to see if the center is soft; if not, add more water (if needed) and bring to a boil again using high heat. When the croquettes are soft, remove them from water; allow to cool down. Once cool sufficient to hold, press each croquette between the palms of your hands to squeeze out all the surplus water.

3. Put in the croquettes to the yogurt and mix softly until all croquettes are coated thoroughly with the yogurt. Garnish with the rest of the 1 teaspoon cumin, green chile pepper, and cilantro before you serve.

Raita with Chickpea Flour Pancakes

Servings: 4 to 6 servings

INGREDIENTS:

- ✓ ⅛ teaspoon baking soda
- ✓ ⅛ teaspoon salt, or to taste
- ✓ ¼ cup chickpea flour
- ✓ ¼ cup water
- ✓ 1 fresh green chile pepper, such as serrano, minced with seeds
- ✓ 1 tablespoon finely chopped fresh cilantro, including soft stems
- ✓ 1 tablespoon minced fresh mint leaves
- ✓ 1 to 2 tablespoons peanut oil
- ✓ 2 cups non-fat plain yogurt, whisked until the desired smoothness is achieved
- ✓ 2 tablespoons minced scallions, white parts only
- ✓ 2 teaspoons Punjabi Raita and Buttermilk Masala

DIRECTIONS:

1. Ready the masala. Next, in a small-sized container, combine the chickpea flour, baking soda, salt, scallions, cilantro, and green chile pepper. Put in

the water to make a semi-thin batter. Set aside for approximately half an hour to rest.

2. Heat 1 teaspoon of the oil in a moderate-sized non-stick skillet over moderate heat. Add approximately 2 tablespoons of the batter and spread it using a spatula to make a 3-inch pancake. When the bottom turns golden, approximately one minute, turn it over and slide it toward the side of the pan, making room for others. Make similar pancakes with the rest of the batter, starting in the center and moving out the side after the first side turns golden. Add more oil, as needed.

3. When the bottoms of the pancakes at the side of the pan brown, approximately one minute, turn them over and let the other side brown, approximately half a minute, then remove to a plate. Break each pancake into ½-inch pieces and set aside.

4. In a serving container, combine the yogurt, raita masala, and the pancake pieces. Garnish with the mint and serve.

Ground Lamb Raita

This recipe is called "Gosht ka raita" in Hindi

Servings:4 to 6 servings

INGREDIENTS:

- ✓ ¼ cup dried yellow split chickpeas (channa dal), sorted and washed in 3 to 4 changes of water
- ✓ ¼ teaspoon salt, or to taste
- ✓ ½ cup finely chopped fresh cilantro, including soft stems
- ✓ 1 cup finely chopped onion
- ✓ 1 cup trimmed and ground leg of lamb
- ✓ 1 fresh green chile pepper, such as serrano, minced with seeds
- ✓ 1 large clove fresh garlic, minced
- ✓ 1 tablespoon peeled minced fresh ginger
- ✓ 2 teaspoons ground coriander
- ✓ 2 teaspoons Kashmiri Raita Masala
- ✓ 4 cups non-fat plain yogurt, whisked until the desired smoothness is achieved

DIRECTIONS:

1. Immerse the dal in water to cover, 1 hour. In the meantime, ready the raita masala. Next, place 3

cups of the yogurt in a big serving container. Stir in 1½ teaspoons of the raita masala. Reserve.

2. Drain the dal, then place it and the lamb, onion, garlic, cilantro, ginger, green chile pepper, coriander, and salt in a small-sized non-stick skillet and cook, stirring, using moderate to high heat until the lamb and onions brown, approximately five minutes. Put in the rest of the 1 cup yogurt and cook, stirring until the lamb and dal become soft, approximately twenty minutes.

3. Allow to cool, move to the container with the yogurt and masala, and mix thoroughly. Garnish with the rest of the ½ teaspoon raita masala and serve.

Shredded Chicken Raita

Servings:4 to 6 servings

INGREDIENTS:

- ✓ ½ recipe Pan-Cooked Chile-Chicken Thighs
- ✓ 2 cups non-fat plain yogurt, whisked until the desired smoothness is achieved
- ✓ 2 to 3 tablespoons Crushed Lemon and Fresh Red Chile Pepper Pickle
- ✓ 2 to 3 tablespoons snipped chives

DIRECTIONS:

1. Ready the pickle in advance. Ready the chicken. Shred the chicken pieces by hand or simply mince them into a food processor and set aside.

2. Put the yogurt in a big serving container and stir in the lemon pickle. Put in the chicken and mix thoroughly. Put in the chives and stir mildly to combine, with some of them visible as a decoration. Serve.

Chopped Salad Yogurt

Servings:4 to 6 servings

INGREDIENTS:

- ✓ ½ cup finely chopped fresh cilantro, including soft stems
- ✓ 1 fresh green chile pepper, such as serrano, minced with seeds
- ✓ 1 tablespoon grated fresh coconut or shredded unsweetened dried coconut
- ✓ 1 tablespoon peeled minced fresh ginger
- ✓ 1 teaspoon black mustard seeds
- ✓ 1 teaspoon cumin seeds
- ✓ 1 teaspoon dried white urad beans (dhulli urad dal)
- ✓ 1 teaspoon dried yellow split chickpeas (channa dal)
- ✓ 1 teaspoon salt, or to taste
- ✓ 2 cups non-fat plain yogurt (do not whisk)
- ✓ 2 tablespoons minced fresh curry leaves
- ✓ 2 teaspoons peanut oil
- ✓ 3 cups finely chopped mixed fresh vegetables, such as tomato, red and daikon radishes, cucumber, scallion, jicama, and zucchini

✓ A scant pinch ground asafoetida

DIRECTIONS:

1. Put the chopped vegetables in a flat serving dish and stir in the cilantro, ginger, coconut, green chile pepper, and salt. Next, lightly fold in the yogurt.

2. Heat the oil in a small-sized non-stick saucepan using moderate to high heat and put in the cumin and mustard seeds; they should splatter when they touch the hot oil, so cover the pan and reduce the heat until the spluttering diminishes. Swiftly add both the dals, the asafoetida, and the curry leaves, and stir until the dals are golden, approximately one minute. Move the seasonings to the yogurt and stir mildly to combine, leaving most of it visible as a decoration. Serve.

Cucumber Pachadi

Servings:4 to 6 servings

INGREDIENTS:

✓ ¼ teaspoon salt, or to taste

✓ ½ cup finely chopped fresh cilantro, including soft stems

✓ ½ teaspoon black mustard seeds

✓ ½ teaspoon cumin seeds

✓ 1 to 2 teaspoons peanut oil

✓ 2 cups non-fat plain yogurt (do not whisk)

✓ 2 to 3 fresh green chile peppers, such as serrano, cut in half along the length and seeded

✓ 3 small seedless cucumbers, peeled and grated

✓ 8 fresh green curry leaves

DIRECTIONS:

1. Put the cucumbers, cilantro, and salt in a serving container, and fold in the yogurt until just incorporated.

2. Heat the oil in a small-sized non-stick saucepan using moderate to high heat and put in the cumin and mustard seeds; they should splutter when they touch the hot oil, so cover the pan and reduce the heat until the spluttering diminishes. Add 5 of the

curry leaves and the green chile peppers and stir approximately one minute. Move the seasonings to the yogurt container and fold in gently. Lightly crumble the rest of the 3 curry leaves to release their aroma, and put them in to the pachadi as a decoration. Serve.

Green Papaya and Coconut Pachadi

Servings:4 to 6 servings

INGREDIENTS:

- ✓ ⅛ teaspoon ground asafoetida
- ✓ ⅛ teaspoon ground paprika
- ✓ ¼ teaspoon ground black mustard seeds
- ✓ ½ cup crudely chopped fresh cilantro, including soft stems
- ✓ ½ cup grated fresh or frozen coconut
- ✓ ½ teaspoon salt, or to taste
- ✓ 1 small seedless cucumber, grated
- ✓ 1 small unripe green papaya, peeled and grated to make 1 cup
- ✓ 1 teaspoon black mustard seeds
- ✓ 1 teaspoon peanut oil
- ✓ 1 teaspoon sugar
- ✓ 1 to 2 dried red chile peppers, such as chile de arbol, crudely broken
- ✓ 1 to 3 fresh green chile peppers, such as serrano, crudely chopped
- ✓ 2 cups non-fat plain yogurt (do not whisk)
- ✓ 2 quarter-size slices peeled fresh ginger

✓ 2 small carrots, grated

DIRECTIONS:

1. In a small food processor, combine and pulse the coconut, cilantro, ginger, green chile peppers, sugar, salt, and ground mustard seeds, adding approximately ¼ cup of the yogurt until a smooth paste is achieved.

2. Put the yogurt in a serving dish and very lightly stir in first the coconut paste, then the papaya, cucumber, and carrots, leaving a few vegetables showing their color through the yogurt.

3. Heat the oil in a small saucepan using moderate to high heat and cook the red chile peppers and mustard seeds; they should splutter when they touch the hot oil, so reduce the heat and cover the pan until the spluttering diminishes. Put in the asafoetida and paprika, then move the seasonings to the pachadi and stir it in, leaving some visible as a decoration. Serve.

Green Tomato Chutney Pachadi

Servings:_4 to 6 servings

INGREDIENTS:

- ✓ 1 small onion, crudely chopped
- ✓ 1 tablespoon black mustard seeds
- ✓ 1 tablespoon peanut oil
- ✓ 1 teaspoon salt, or to taste
- ✓ 1 teaspoon South Indian Sambar Powder (Homemade or store-bought)
- ✓ 1 to 3 fresh green chile peppers, such as serrano, crudely chopped with seeds
- ✓ 2 cups non-fat plain yogurt (do not whisk)
- ✓ 2 large firm green tomatoes, crudely chopped
- ✓ 2 tablespoons Tamarind Paste (Homemade or store-bought)
- ✓ 8 to 10 fresh curry leaves

DIRECTIONS:

1. Ready the tamarind paste and sambar powder. Next, heat the oil in a big non-stick wok or saucepan using moderate to high heat and put in the mustard seeds; they should splutter when they touch the hot oil, so cover the pan and reduce the heat until the spluttering diminishes. Swiftly put in

the green chile peppers, tomatoes, and onion, and cook, stirring, until the tomatoes are golden, approximately three minutes. Turn off the heat and allow to cool down.

2. Move to a food processor or blender, put in the tamarind, curry leaves, and salt, and process to make a smooth chutney.

3. Put the yogurt in a serving container and fold in the chutney, with parts of it visible as a decoration. Top with the sambar powder and serve.

Mango and Coconut Pachadi

Servings:4 to 6 servings

INGREDIENTS:

✓ ½ teaspoon salt, or to taste

✓ 1 fresh green chile pepper, such as serrano, minced with seeds

✓ 1 large semi-ripe mango, peeled and cut into ½-inch pieces

✓ 1 tablespoon dried coconut powder (kopra) or unsweetened shredded dried coconut

✓ 1 tablespoon peeled minced fresh ginger

✓ 1 teaspoon black mustard seeds

✓ 1 teaspoon peanut oil

✓ 1½ cups non-fat plain yogurt (do not whisk)

✓ 2 dried red chile peppers, such as chile de arbol, broken

✓ 5 to 7 fresh curry leaves

✓ A scant pinch ground asafoetida

DIRECTIONS:

1. Put the mango pieces in a serving container and cautiously stir in the coconut powder (or dried

coconut), ginger, green chile pepper, and salt. Next, fold in the yogurt.

2. Heat the oil in a small-sized non-stick saucepan using moderate to high heat and put in the red chile peppers and mustard seeds; they should splutter when they touch the hot oil, so cover the pan and reduce the heat until the spluttering diminishes. Swiftly put in the asafoetida and curry leaves and stir for approximately half a minute. Move to the yogurt and stir mildly to combine, leaving most of it visible on top as a decoration. Serve.

Mashed Potato and Cilantro Pachadi

Servings:4 to 6 servings

INGREDIENTS:

✓ ⅛ teaspoon ground asafoetida

✓ ¼ teaspoon ground turmeric

✓ ½ cup finely chopped fresh cilantro, including soft stems

✓ ½ teaspoon crudely ground black pepper

✓ ½ teaspoon fenugreek seeds, crudely ground

✓ 1 cup non-fat plain yogurt (do not whisk)

✓ 1 fresh green chile pepper, such as serrano, minced with seeds

✓ 1 pound russet (or boiling) potatoes

✓ 1 tablespoon peanut oil

✓ 1 teaspoon black mustard seeds

✓ 1 teaspoon cumin seeds

✓ 1 teaspoon dried yellow split chickpeas (channa dal)

✓ 1 teaspoon salt, or to taste

✓ 3 dried red chile peppers, such as chile de arbol, with stems

✓ 5 to 7 fresh curry leaves

DIRECTIONS:

1. Boil the potatoes in lightly salted water to cover until soft, approximately twenty minutes. Allow to cool, then peel and mash them crudely with a fork.

2. Heat 1 teaspoon oil in a moderate-sized non-stick wok or saucepan using moderate to high heat and put in the cumin, fenugreek, black pepper, and asafoetida. Stir approximately half a minute. Put in the mashed potatoes, green chile pepper, turmeric, and salt, and cook, stirring, using moderate to high heat until heated through, approximately two minutes. Decrease the heat to low, cover the pan, and cook, stirring intermittently, approximately ten minutes.

3. Allow to cool to room temperature. Move to a serving container and fold in the yogurt until just incorporated. Lightly stir in the cilantro.

4. Heat the rest of the oil in a small-sized non-stick saucepan using moderate to high heat and put in the red chile peppers and mustard seeds; they should splutter when they touch the hot oil, so cover the pan and reduce the heat until the spluttering diminishes. Swiftly put in the dal and curry leaves and stir until a golden colour is

achieved, approximately half a minute. Move to the yogurt container and stir mildly to combine, leaving most of it visible as a decoration. Serve.

Pumpkin and Tamarind Pachadi

Servings:4 to 6 servings

INGREDIENTS:

✓ ⅛ teaspoon ground asafoetida

✓ ½ cup finely chopped fresh cilantro, including soft stems

✓ ½ teaspoon black peppercorns, crudely ground

✓ cup non-fat plain yogurt, whisked until the desired smoothness is achieved

✓ fresh green chile pepper, such as serrano, minced with seeds

✓ pound pumpkin or any other orange squash, peeled and cut into ½-inch pieces

✓ tablespoon peanut oil

✓ teaspoon black mustard seeds

✓ teaspoon dried coconut powder

✓ teaspoon fenugreek seeds, crudely ground

✓ teaspoon melted ghee

✓ 1 teaspoon salt, or to taste

✓ teaspoons dried tamarind powder

✓ whole dried red chile peppers, such as chile de arbol

DIRECTIONS:

1. Heat the oil in a moderate-sized non-stick saucepan using moderate to high heat then put in

the fenugreek, black peppercorns, and asafoetida; stir for approximately half a minute. Stir in the pumpkin, green chile pepper, and salt, and cook, stirring, using moderate to high heat until heated through, approximately two minutes. Decrease the heat to low, cover the pan and cook, stirring intermittently, until the pumpkin is soft, 20 to 30 minutes.

2. Put in the tamarind and coconut during the last 5 minutes of cooking. When completely cooked, stir in the cilantro and allow to cool down to room temperature. Move to a serving container and fold in the yogurt until just incorporated.

3. Heat the ghee in a small-sized non-stick saucepan using moderate to high heat and put in the red chile peppers and mustard seeds; they should splutter when they touch the hot oil, so cover the pan and reduce the heat until the spluttering diminishes. Swiftly move to the yogurt container, mix lightly before you serve.

Rice Flakes Pachadi

Servings:4 to 6 servings

INGREDIENTS:

- ✓ ⅛ teaspoon ground asafoetida
- ✓ ¼ cup finely chopped fresh cilantro, including soft stems
- ✓ ¼ teaspoon ground paprika
- ✓ ¼ teaspoon salt, or to taste
- ✓ ½ teaspoon black mustard seeds
- ✓ 1 cup pressed rice flakes (poha), sorted
- ✓ 1 fresh green chile pepper, such as serrano, minced with seeds
- ✓ 1 tablespoon grated fresh or frozen coconut or shredded unsweetened dried coconut
- ✓ 1 teaspoon coconut or peanut oil
- ✓ 2 cups non-fat plain yogurt, whisked until the desired smoothness is achieved
- ✓ 6 to 8 fresh curry leaves

DIRECTIONS:

1. In a skillet, dry-roast the rice flakes, coconut, cilantro, and green chile pepper over moderate heat until it begins to look golden and releases its

fragrance, approximately two minutes. Put the yogurt in a serving container and stir in the roasted rice flakes mixture and salt.

2. Heat the oil in a small saucepan using moderate to high heat and put in the curry leaves and mustard seeds; they should splutter when they touch the hot oil, so reduce the heat and cover the pan until the spluttering diminishes. Mix in the paprika and asafoetida, then instantly move the seasonings to the yogurt and stir mildly to combine, with parts of it visible as a decoration. Serve.

Sautéed Banana Pachadi

Servings:4 to 6 servings

INGREDIENTS:

- ✓ ⅛ teaspoon ground asafoetida
- ✓ ¼ cup grated fresh or frozen coconut
- ✓ ¼ teaspoon + ½ teaspoon salt, or to taste
- ✓ ½ teaspoon fenugreek seeds
- ✓ ½ teaspoon freshly ground black pepper, or to taste
- ✓ 1 tablespoon dried curry leaves
- ✓ 1 tablespoon peanut oil
- ✓ 1 teaspoon black mustard seeds
- ✓ 1 teaspoon cumin seeds
- ✓ 1 teaspoon hot red pepper flakes, or to taste
- ✓ 2 medium firm ripe bananas, peeled and cut into ¼-inch pieces
- ✓ 2 to 3 tablespoons fresh lemon juice
- ✓ 3 cups non-fat plain yogurt, whisked until the desired smoothness is achieved

DIRECTIONS:

1. In a serving container, combine the yogurt, coconut, ¼ teaspoon salt, and black pepper. In a

spice or a coffee grinder, mix together and grind the mustard, cumin, and fenugreek seeds, and the asafoetida, curry leaves, and red pepper flakes until fine.

2. Heat the oil in a big non-stick wok or saucepan using moderate to high heat and put in the ground spice mixture; it should sizzle instantly. Swiftly put in the bananas and ½ teaspoon salt and cook, flipping the pieces carefully, until a golden colour is achieved on both sides, approximately three minutes.

3. Stir in the lemon juice and cook another minute. Move the seasoned bananas to the yogurt and stir mildly to combine, with parts of them visible as a decoration. Refrigerate at least two hours to chill, then serve.

Sautéed Tomatoes and Coconut Pachadi

Servings:4 to 6 servings

INGREDIENTS:

✓ ¼ cup finely chopped fresh cilantro, including soft stems

✓ ¼ cup fresh or frozen grated coconut or unsweetened shredded coconut

✓ ½ cup Coconut Milk (Homemade or store-bought)

✓ ½ teaspoon salt, or to taste

✓ 1 tablespoon peanut or coconut oil

✓ 1 tablespoon peeled minced fresh ginger

✓ 1 teaspoon black mustard seeds

✓ 1 teaspoon cumin seeds

✓ 1 teaspoon dried yellow split chickpeas (channa dal)

✓ 1 to 3 fresh green chile peppers, such as serrano, minced with seeds

✓ 2 cups non-fat plain yogurt (do not whisk)

✓ 2 large tomatoes, crudely chopped

✓ 3 dried red chile peppers, such as chile de arbol, with stems

✓ 8 to 10 fresh curry leaves

DIRECTIONS:

1. Ready the coconut milk. Next, in a serving container, lightly combine the yogurt, coconut milk, ginger, cilantro, green chile peppers, coconut, and salt. (It should not be smooth.)

2. Heat the oil in a small-sized non-stick saucepan using moderate to high heat and put in the red chile peppers, dal, mustard and cumin seeds; they should splutter when they touch the hot oil, so cover the pan and reduce the heat until the spluttering diminishes. Swiftly put in the curry leaves and stir for approximately half a minute. Put in the tomatoes and cook, stirring, until tender, approximately two minutes, then fold everything into the yogurt. Serve.

Tomato and Cucumber Pachadi

Servings:4 to 6 servings

INGREDIENTS:

- ✓ four to five small seedless cucumbers, peeled and finely chopped
- ✓ ¼ teaspoon salt, or to taste
- ✓ ½ cup finely chopped fresh cilantro, including soft stems
- ✓ ½ teaspoon cumin seeds
- ✓ 1 large tomato, finely chopped
- ✓ 1 teaspoon black mustard seeds
- ✓ 1 teaspoon dried yellow split chickpeas (channa dal)
- ✓ 1 teaspoon peanut oil
- ✓ 2 cups non-fat plain yogurt (do not whisk)
- ✓ 2 tablespoons minced fresh curry leaves
- ✓ 2 to 3 fresh green chile peppers, such as serrano, cut in half along the length and seeded
- ✓ A few fresh cilantro leaves
- ✓ A scant pinch ground asafoetida

DIRECTIONS:

1. Put the cucumbers, tomato, cilantro, and salt in a serving container and fold in the yogurt until just incorporated.

2. Heat the oil in a small-sized non-stick saucepan using moderate to high heat and put in the mustard seeds; they should splutter when they touch the hot oil, so cover the pan and reduce the heat until the spluttering diminishes. Swiftly put in the dal and stir until a golden colour is achieved, approximately half a minute, then put in the cumin seeds, curry leaves, and asafoetida and stir another half a minute. Move the seasonings into the yogurt container and fold in gently. Garnish with the green chile peppers and cilantro leaves before you serve.

Tomato, Cucumber, and Onion Yogurt

Servings:4 to 6 servings

<u>INGREDIENTS:</u>

- ✓ four to five small seedless cucumbers, peeled and finely chopped
- ✓ ½ cup finely chopped fresh cilantro, including soft stems + extra for garnish
- ✓ ½ teaspoon salt, or to taste
- ✓ 1 large tomato, finely chopped
- ✓ 1 small white onion, cut in half along the length and thinly chopped
- ✓ 1 tablespoon minced fresh curry leaves
- ✓ 1 tablespoon peeled minced fresh ginger
- ✓ 1 teaspoon black mustard seeds
- ✓ 1 teaspoon cumin seeds
- ✓ 1 teaspoon dried yellow split chickpeas (channa dal)
- ✓ 1 teaspoon dried yellow split pigeon peas (toor dal)
- ✓ 1 teaspoon peanut oil
- ✓ 1½ cups non-fat plain yogurt (do not whisk)
- ✓ 2 dried red chile peppers, such as chile de arbol, crudely broken

✓ 2 fresh green chile peppers, such as serrano, diagonally chopped thin ½ teaspoon ground fenugreek seeds

✓ 2 tablespoons finely chopped fresh cilantro, including soft stems

DIRECTIONS:

1. Put the cucumbers, tomato, onion, cilantro, and salt in a serving container and fold in the yogurt until just incorporated.

2. Heat the oil in a small-sized non-stick saucepan using moderate to high heat and put in the red chile peppers and ginger, stir a few seconds, then put in the cumin and mustard seeds; they should splutter when they touch the hot oil, so cover the pan and reduce the heat until the spluttering diminishes. Swiftly add both dals, curry leaves, green chile peppers, and fenugreek, and stir until a golden colour is achieved, approximately one minute. Move seasoning into the yogurt container and fold it in gently. Garnish with the cilantro leaves and serve.

Potato and Cashew Tikki

Servings:4 to 6 servings

INGREDIENTS

- ✓ ¼ teaspoon crudely ground ajwain seeds
- ✓ ¼ teaspoon cayenne pepper, or to taste
- ✓ ½ cup crudely chopped raw cashews
- ✓ ½ teaspoon salt, or to taste
- ✓ 1 tablespoon ground coriander
- ✓ 1 tablespoon peeled minced fresh ginger
- ✓ 1 teaspoon **Chaat Masala** (Homemade or store-bought)
- ✓ 1 teaspoon dried fenugreek leaves
- ✓ 1 teaspoon fresh green chile pepper, such as serrano, minced with seeds
- ✓ 1½ to 2 cups peanut oil for deep-frying
- ✓ 2 large eggs, lightly beaten
- ✓ 2 large russet (or any) potatoes (about 1 pound)

DIRECTIONS:

1. Ready the chaat masala. Cook the potatoes in lightly salted boiling water to cover until tender, approximately twenty minutes. Cool, then peel and mash. In a large container, put in the mashed potatoes, ginger, green chile pepper, coriander,

fenugreek, ajwain, cayenne pepper, and salt. With clean hands, softly mix everything together. (Don't use a food processor; over-mixing will result in glutinous potatoes.)

2. With mildly greased hands, divide the mixture into 20 portions and shape each one into a round ball, then flatten lightly to make a smooth patty or an oval.

3. Heat the oil in a big wok or skillet until it reaches 350°F to 375°F on a frying thermometer or until a small piece of the mixture dropped into the hot oil bubbles and instantly rises to the top. Dip each patty in the beaten egg, then cover thoroughly with the cashews.

4. Heat the oil in a big wok or skillet until it reaches 350°F to 375°F on a frying thermometer or until a small piece of the potato mixture dropped into the hot oil bubbles and instantly rises to the top. Put in the potato ovals into the hot oil cautiously using your fingers or a spoon to avoid spluttering. Add as many as the wok can hold simultaneously without crowding and fry each batch, turning a few times with a slotted spatula, until crunchy and golden on all sides, approximately one to two minutes.

5. Move to paper towels to drain. Repeat the process with the rest of the ovals. Drain using paper towels, garnish with the chaat masala before you serve.

Potato and Tapioca Tikki

Servings:15 to 20 pieces

INGREDIENTS:

- ✓ ¼ cup minced fresh spinach leaves
- ✓ ⅓ cup tapioca pearls
- ✓ ½ cup boiling water
- ✓ ½ teaspoon garam masala
- ✓ ½ teaspoon ground cumin
- ✓ 1 tablespoon ground coriander
- ✓ 1 tablespoon peeled minced fresh ginger
- ✓ 1 to 2 tablespoons plain dried bread crumbs, if required
- ✓ 1½ to 2 cups peanut oil for frying
- ✓ 2 large russet (or any) potatoes (about 1 pound)
- ✓ 4 to 6 scallions, white parts only, minced

DIRECTIONS:

1. In a small pan, soak 1 tablespoon of the tapioca in the boiling water for approximately half an hour. In the meantime, cook the potatoes in lightly salted boiling water to cover until tender, approximately twenty minutes. Drain, allow to cool down, then peel and mash.

2. In a small pan, cook the soaked tapioca over moderate heat until it turns glutinous, approximately five minutes. (You will still see the grain.) Allow to cool. Crudely grind the rest of the tapioca in a coffee or spice grinder. Move to a flat dish and set aside for coating the patties.

3. In a container, put in the mashed potatoes, ginger, scallions, spinach, coriander, cumin, garam masala, and the cooked tapioca. With clean hands, softly mix everything together. (Don't use a food processor; over-mixing will result in glutinous potatoes.) If the mixture appears too soft, stir in 1 to 2 tablespoons of bread crumbs.

4. With mildly greased hands, divide the potato mixture into 20 portions and shape each one into a round ball, then flatten lightly to make a smooth disc or oval. Coat each disc with the ground tapioca, then press between the palms of your hands to ensure that the tapioca adheres nicely.

5. Heat the oil in a big wok or skillet until it reaches 350°F to 375°F on a frying thermometer or until a small piece of the potato mixture dropped into the hot oil bubbles and instantly rises to the top. Put in the potato ovals into the hot oil cautiously using

your fingers or a spoon to avoid spluttering. Add as many as the wok can hold simultaneously without crowding and fry each batch, turning a few times with a slotted spatula, until crunchy and golden on all sides, approximately one to two minutes.

6. Move to paper towels to drain. Repeat the process with the rest of the ovals. Move to a serving platter and serve hot.

Tofu and Potato Tikki

Servings: 8 to 10 pieces

INGREDIENTS:

- ✓ ¼ cup peanut or vegetable oil
- ✓ ¼ teaspoon salt, or to taste
- ✓ 1 (10½-ounce) package firm tofu, crumbled and dried well on paper towels
- ✓ 1 fresh green chile pepper, such as serrano, stemmed
- ✓ 1 large russet (or any) potato
- ✓ 2 quarter-size slices peeled fresh ginger
- ✓ Freshly ground black pepper, to taste

DIRECTIONS:

1. Cook the potato in lightly salted boiling water to cover until tender, approximately fifteen minutes. Drain, allow to cool down, peel, place in a moderate-sized container, and mash.

2. Using a food processor, combine and pulse the chile pepper and ginger until minced, then put in the tofu and pulse a few times until the desired smoothness is achieved. Put in the tofu mixture to the potatoes, along with salt and black pepper and, with clean hands, softly mix everything together.

(Don't use your food processor for this; over-mixing will result in glutinous potatoes.)

3. With mildly greased hands, divide the mixture into 8 to 10 portions and shape each one into a smooth 1½- to 2-inch patty.

4. Heat 3 tablespoons of the oil in a large, heavy, non-stick skillet using moderate to high heat. Put the patties in the skillet in a single layer, in batches if required. Press on them lightly using a spatula, ensuring all the edges are in contact with the skillet. Let cook undisturbed approximately one minute, reduce the heat to moderate to low and continue to cook, watching cautiously until the bottom side is golden, approximately five minutes.

5. Cautiously turn each tikki over with the spatula. Add 1 to 2 tablespoons more oil (if required) and increase the heat to high approximately a minute. Next, reduce the heat to moderate to low once again and cook until the second side is golden, approximately four to five minutes. Reduce the heat and push the patties to the sides of the pan until they are thoroughly browned and a have a thick, crunchy crust. Turn a few times, as required.

6. Another way is to deep-fry the patties in hot oil and then finish cooking them on a tava-griddle. (If, when you deep-fry, the patties seem to open up or disintegrate, make a paste with ¼ cup all-purpose flour and ¼ cup water and coat rest of the patties in it before deep-frying.) Serve hot.

Coconut–Red Chile Croquettes

Servings: 20 to 25 pieces

INGREDIENTS:

- ✓ ¼ cup each: split pigeon peas (toor dal), yellow split chickpeas (channa dal), white urad beans (dhulli urad dal), sorted and washed in 3 to 4 changes of water
- ✓ ¼ cup finely chopped fresh cilantro, including soft stems
- ✓ ¼ teaspoon baking powder
- ✓ ¼ teaspoon ground asafoetida
- ✓ ¼ to ½ cup hot water
- ✓ ⅓ cup non-fat plain yogurt
- ✓ ½ cup rice flour
- ✓ ½ to 1 cup finely chopped onions
- ✓ 1 cup grated fresh or frozen coconut or shredded unsweetened dried coconut
- ✓ 1 teaspoon salt, or to taste
- ✓ 1 to 3 fresh green chile peppers, such as serrano, minced without seeds
- ✓ 1½ to 2 cups peanut oil for deep-frying
- ✓ 2 tablespoons peeled minced fresh ginger
- ✓ 2 to 4 dried red chile peppers, such as chile de arbol, crudely ground

DIRECTIONS:

1. Immerse the dals in water to cover by 1 inch, approximately 3 hours. Drain and move to a food processor. Process until thoroughly smooth. Put in the rice flour, coconut, and yogurt, and process once more until the desired smoothness is achieved. Move to a container. Add all the rest of the ingredients (except the oil for frying) and mix thoroughly, adding the hot water as required to make a fluffy, thick batter that can be shaped.

2. Heat the oil in a big wok or skillet to 350°F to 375°F on a frying thermometer or until a pinch of batter dropped into the hot oil bubbles and instantly rises to the top.

3. With lightly moistened clean hands, shape the batter put them in carefully, one at a time, to the hot oil. Add as many as the wok can hold simultaneously without crowding, and fry, turning once in a while using tongs or a slotted spoon, until they are crisp and golden on all sides, approximately two to three minutes. (Dip your fingers in the container of water as you work.) Move croquettes to paper towels to drain. Move to a platter and serve hot.

Mung Croquettes

Servings: 18 to 20 pieces

INGREDIENTS:

✓ ⅛ teaspoon baking soda

✓ ½ teaspoon salt, or to taste

✓ 1 cup dried yellow mung beans (dhulli mung dal), sorted and washed in 3 to 4 changes of water

✓ 1 fresh green chile pepper, such as serrano, stemmed

✓ 1 to 3 tablespoons hot water

✓ 1½ to 2 cups peanut oil for deep-frying

✓ 3 quarter-size slices peeled fresh ginger

DIRECTIONS:

1. Immerse the dal overnight in water to cover by 2 inches. Drain. Using a food processor, combine and pulse the ginger and green chile pepper until minced. Put in the drained dal and process, adding the hot water as required to make a fluffy, semi-thick batter that can be shaped. Stir in the salt and baking soda.

2. Heat the oil in a big wok or a skillet to 350°F to 375°F on a frying thermometer or until a pinch of batter dropped into the hot oil bubbles and

93

instantly rises to the top. Pick up approximately 2 tablespoons of the batter using clean fingers or a spoon and push it cautiously into the hot oil. (Don't worry approximately the shape when you slide it into the oil.) Add as many croquettes as the wok will hold simultaneously without crowding, and fry, turning with a slotted spoon, until they are crunchy and golden on all sides, approximately two to three minutes.

3. Using a slotted spatula, move croquettes to paper towels to drain. Repeat process with the remaining batter. Move to a platter and serve hot or at room temperature.

Rice Croquettes

Servings: *20 pieces*

<u>INGREDIENTS:</u>

- ✓ ¼ teaspoon baking soda
- ✓ ¼ teaspoon ground asafoetida
- ✓ ¼ to ½ cup hot water
- ✓ ⅓ cup crudely chopped cashews
- ✓ ½ cup dried white urad beans (dhulli urad dal), sorted and washed in 3 to 4 changes of water
- ✓ ½ teaspoon salt, or to taste
- ✓ 1 cup long-grain white rice, sorted and washed in 3 to 4 changes of water
- ✓ 1 small 3-inch diameter container
- ✓ 1 tablespoon peanut oil
- ✓ 1 teaspoon crudely ground fenugreek seeds
- ✓ 1 teaspoon black mustard seeds
- ✓ 1½ to 2 cups peanut oil for deep-frying
- ✓ 2 tablespoons dried yellow split chickpeas (channa dal)
- ✓ 2 tablespoons minced fresh curry leaves
- ✓ One 10-inch square piece of plastic wrap

DIRECTIONS:

1. Setting aside 2 tablespoons of the rice, soak the rice and dal in water to cover by 2 inches, approximately four hours. Drain and move to a food processor and process, adding hot water as required to make a fluffy, semi-thick batter that can be shaped. Put in the baking soda and salt, and process once more. Move to a container.

2. Heat 1 tablespoon oil in a big cast-iron or non-stick wok or a saucepan, using moderate to high heat and put in the mustard seeds. They should splutter when they touch the hot oil, so cover the pan and reduce the heat until the spluttering diminishes. Swiftly put in the reserved 2 tablespoons rice, chickpea dal, fenugreek seeds, asafoetida, curry leaves, and cashews, and cook, stirring, until a golden colour is achieved, approximately one minute. Combine with the batter. Cover and let rest in a warm, draft-free place approximately two hours.

3. Heat the oil for frying in a big wok or skillet to 350°F to 375°F on a frying thermometer, or until a pinch of batter dropped into the hot oil bubbles and instantly rises to the top.

4. In the meantime, have ready a small-sized container of water. Wrap a small piece of plastic wrap tautly around the 3-inch container and brush with a light coating of oil. Put 1 tablespoon of the batter on the wrap and with lightly moistened, clean fingers, spread the batter into a 3-inch disc. With your forefinger, make a ½-inch hole in the center of the disc to make a doughnut shape. Gently slide each doughnut to the side and into the hot oil. (Dip your fingers in a container of water as you work.)

5. Deep-fry, adding 3 to 4 croquettes at a time and turning them using tongs 2 to 3 times until puffed and golden, approximately three minutes per batch. Move to paper towels to drain. Move to a platter and serve hot.

Salty Croquettes

Servings: 10 to 12 pieces

INGREDIENTS:

- ✓ ¼ teaspoon baking soda
- ✓ ¼ to ⅓ cup water
- ✓ ½ teaspoon ground asafoetida
- ✓ ½ teaspoon salt, or to taste
- ✓ 1 (10-inch-square) piece of muslin or 4 layers cheesecloth
- ✓ 1 (10-inch-square) piece of plastic wrap
- ✓ 1 cup dried white urad beans (dhulli urad dal), sorted and washed in 3 to 4 changes of water
- ✓ 1 small 3-inch diameter container
- ✓ 1 tablespoon shelled and crudely ground raw almonds
- ✓ 1 teaspoon cumin seeds
- ✓ 1 to 3 fresh green chile peppers, such as serrano, stemmed
- ✓ 1½ to 2 cups peanut oil for deep-frying
- ✓ 2 tablespoons chopped raisins
- ✓ 3 tablespoons shelled and crudely ground raw pistachios
- ✓ 5 to 7 quarter-size slices peeled fresh ginger

DIRECTIONS:

1. Immerse the dal overnight in water to cover by 2-inches. Drain. Using a food processor, process the ginger and green chile peppers until minced. Put in the drained dal and the water as required, and process until thoroughly smooth. Stir in the cumin seeds, asafoetida, baking soda, and salt. (The batter should be thick and slightly grainy. If it appears thin, add some chickpea flour. You should actually be able to pick up this batter using your fingers to stuff it and shape it.)

2. Move to a container, cover, and keep in a warm, draft-free place approximately eight to ten hours to ferment. Next, using a whisk or a fork, whisk the batter to that it absorbs air and becomes fluffy, approximately three minutes.

3. In a small-sized container, combine the pistachios, raisins, and almonds. Next, heat the oil in a big wok or skillet to 350°F to 375°F on a frying thermometer, or until a pinch of batter dropped into the hot oil bubbles and instantly rises to the top.

4. Have ready another small-sized container of water. Wrap a small piece of plastic wrap tautly around a

3-inch container and brush lightly with oil. Put ½ tablespoon of the batter on the wrap and, with lightly moistened clean fingers, spread it into a 3-inch semicircle. Put approximately 1 teaspoon of the nut mixture in the center of the semicircle. Cover the filling with another tablespoon of the batter and lightly press the top batter into the bottom, sealing in the filling, maintaining the shape. With your hands or a slotted spoon, slide the semicircles cautiously into the hot oil. If the batter sticks to your fingers, dip your hands in the container of water as you go along.

5. Deep-fry, adding as many semi-circles as the wok can hold simultaneously without crowding, turning once in a while until they are crisp and golden on all sides, approximately two to three minutes. Using a slotted spatula, move croquettes to paper towels to drain. Repeat the process with the rest of the batter. Move to a platter and serve hot.

South Indian Croquettes

Servings: 15 to 20 pieces

INGREDIENTS:

- ✓ ¼ cup long-grain white rice, sorted and washed in 3 to 4 changes of water
- ✓ ¼ teaspoon baking powder
- ✓ ¼ teaspoon ground asafoetida
- ✓ ¼ to ⅓ cup hot water
- ✓ ½ teaspoon cayenne pepper, or to taste
- ✓ ½ teaspoon ground fenugreek seeds
- ✓ 1 cup dried white urad beans (dhulli urad dal), sorted and washed in 3 to 4 changes of water
- ✓ 1 teaspoon crudely ground black pepper, or to taste
- ✓ 1 teaspoon salt, or to taste
- ✓ 1½ to 2 cups peanut oil for deep-frying
- ✓ 20 to 25 fresh curry leaves
- ✓ 4 quarter-size slices peeled fresh ginger

DIRECTIONS:

1. Immerse together the dal and rice overnight in water to cover by 2-inches. Drain.

2. Using a food processor, combine and pulse the ginger and curry leaves until minced. Put in the

drained dal, rice, fenugreek seeds, asafoetida, and salt, and process, adding hot water as required to make a fluffy, thick batter that can be shaped. Cover and keep in a warm and draft-free place, eight to ten hours to ferment. Stir in the cayenne and black peppers, and the baking powder. Next, using a whisk or a fork, whisk the batter to that it absorbs air and becomes fluffy, approximately one minute.

3. Heat the oil in a big wok or skillet to 350°F to 375°F on a frying thermometer or until a pinch of batter dropped into the hot oil bubbles and instantly rises to the top.

4. In the meantime, have ready a small-sized container of water. With lightly moistened clean hands, form 2-inch patties from the batter and put them in carefully, one at a time, to the hot oil. Add as many as the wok can hold simultaneously without crowding, and fry, turning once in a while using tongs or a slotted spoon, until they are crisp and golden on all sides, approximately two to three minutes. (Dip your fingers in the container of water as you work.) Move croquettes to paper towels to drain. Move to a platter and serve hot.

Spinach Mung Croquettes

Servings: 12 to 15 pieces

INGREDIENTS:

- ✓ ¼ teaspoon baking soda
- ✓ ½ small bunch fresh spinach (four to five ounces), trimmed, washed, and finely chopped
- ✓ ½ teaspoon ajwain seeds, crudely ground
- ✓ ½ teaspoon salt, or to taste
- ✓ 1 cup dried yellow mung beans (dhulli mung dal), sorted and washed in 3 to 4 changes of water
- ✓ 1 large onion, finely chopped
- ✓ 1 tablespoon coriander, crudely ground
- ✓ 1 tablespoon peeled minced fresh ginger
- ✓ 1 teaspoon **Chaat Masala** (Homemade or store-bought)
- ✓ 1 teaspoon cumin seeds, dry-roasted and crudely ground (See the dry-roasting section in Introduction)
- ✓ 1½ to 2 cups peanut oil for deep-frying

DIRECTIONS:

1. Immerse the dal overnight in water to cover by 2-inches. In the meantime, ready the chaat masala and the cumin seeds. When ready, drain and place

the dal Using a food processor, then process, adding the hot water as required to make a fluffy, semi-thick batter that can be shaped. Stir in all the rest of the ingredients (except the spinach and oil) and process once more. Move to a container and stir in the spinach, then allow to rest for approximately half an hour.

2. Heat the oil in a big wok or skillet to 350°F to 375°F on a frying thermometer, or until a pinch of batter dropped into the hot oil bubbles and instantly rises to the top. Pick up approximately 2 tablespoons of the batter with clean fingers or a spoon and push it cautiously into the hot oil. (Don't worry approximately the shape when you slide the croquettes into the oil.) Add as many as the wok will hold simultaneously without crowding, and fry, turning with a slotted spatula, until they are crisp and golden on all sides, approximately two to three minutes.

3. Using a slotted spatula, move croquettes to paper towels to drain. Repeat process with the rest of the batter. Move to a platter, garnish with chaat masala before you serve.

Urad Croquettes

Servings: 10 to 12 pieces

INGREDIENTS:

- ✓ ¼ teaspoon baking soda
- ✓ ¼ teaspoon ground asafoetida
- ✓ ¼ to ⅓ cup hot water
- ✓ 1 (10-inch-square) piece of muslin or 4 layers of cheesecloth
- ✓ 1 cup dried split white urad beans (dhulli urad dal), sorted and washed in 3 to 4 changes of water
- ✓ 1 small 3-inch diameter container
- ✓ 1 tablespoon cumin seeds, dry-roasted and crudely ground (See the dry-roasting section in Introduction)
- ✓ 1 teaspoon salt, or to taste
- ✓ 1 to 3 fresh green chile peppers, such as serrano, stemmed
- ✓ 1½ to 2 cups peanut oil for deep-frying
- ✓ 5 to 7 quarter-size slices peeled fresh ginger

DIRECTIONS:

1. Immerse the dal overnight in water to cover by 2 inches. In the meantime, ready the cumin. When ready, drain the dal. Using a food processor,

combine and pulse the ginger and green chile peppers until minced. Put in the drained dal and process, adding the hot water as required to make a fluffy, thick batter that can be shaped.

2. Stir in the cumin, baking soda, asafoetida, and salt. Cover and keep in a warm, draft-free place, eight to ten hours to ferment. Next, using a whisk or a fork, whisk the batter to that it absorbs air and becomes fluffy, approximately one minute.

3. Heat the oil in a big wok or skillet to 350°F to 375°F on a frying thermometer, or until a pinch of batter dropped into the hot oil bubbles and instantly rises to the top.

4. In the meantime, have ready a small-sized container of water. Wet the cheesecloth with water, squeeze it out completely and wrap it tautly over the top of the container. There will be some overhang. Holding the overhang securely under the container, with a clean hand, place approximately 2 tablespoons of the batter on the cheesecloth and, with lightly moistened fingers, spread it into a 3-inch disc. With your forefinger, make a ½-inch hole in the center of the disc to make a doughnut. Gently push from one side to slide each doughnut

into the hot oil. (Dip your fingers in the container of water as you work.) Add as many doughnuts as the wok can hold simultaneously without crowding and deep-fry, turning once in a while with a slotted spatula until they

Lightning Source UK Ltd.
Milton Keynes UK
UKHW051230090521
383282UK00014B/310